The Jacobites in the Forty-Five

A.D. CAMERON

Oliver & Boyd

OLIVER & BOYD
Robert Stevenson House
1–3 Baxter's Place
Leith Walk
Edinburgh EHI 3BB
A Division of Longman Group Ltd

First published 1977
Fourth impression 1986

ISBN 0 05 003012 4

Produced by Longman Group (FE) Ltd
Printed in Hong Kong

Acknowledgments

The author and publishers wish to thank the following for permission to reproduce materials on the undernoted pages:

His Grace the Duke of Atholl, page 19;

Edinburgh City Libraries, pages 24, 25, 33, 37, 48;

Her Majesty the Queen, page 43;

The Mansell Collection, page 7;

Radio Times Hulton Picture Library, page 22;

Scottish National Portrait Gallery, pages 4, 21, 40, 46;

Scottish United Services Museum, Edinburgh, pages 9, 35, 38;

The Trustees of the National Library of Scotland, pages 40–1;

The Earl of Wemyss and March, K.T., LL.D., page 5

Maps and reconstructions by Tim Smith.

Cover illustration by Donald Harkey

Contents

Introduction

The Old Pretender

The story of the Jacobite risings has often been told. Many writers of history have described the events, and novelists, story-tellers, poets and song-writers also have been inspired by the Jacobite risings.

Looking back from the present day to the rising in 1745, we are able to see what happened, and where, and when, and how it ended. We could read of these events in *History for Young Scots*, Book 2, Chapter 1, for example. It would probably be better to read the first few pages only, and learn what kind of people became Jacobites, what had happened in earlier risings in 1715 and 1719 and why there seemed to be less and less Jacobite feeling as the years passed. That would put us in the same position as people in Britain in the middle of the summer of 1745. They had no idea that Prince Charles Edward Stuart, the son of the Old Pretender, was about to land in Britain and that there would soon be another Jacobite rising. Most people did not even know who he was.

This book does not try just to re-tell a well-known story. 'Bonnie Prince Charlie' is certainly here, but so are a lot of other people of different ranks and occupations. We shall come to know them by looking at the sources they have left—their letters, reports in their newspapers, accounts by their leaders and histories, especially those written near the time by people who were present at the events they described. There we can see what people in different parts of Britain thought and felt and what it really was like to be living then.

The following lines give some idea of the problem people had in understanding what was happening in 1745:

> God bless the King, I mean the Faith's
>   Defender,
> God bless—no harm in blessing—the
>   Pretender,
> But who Pretender is, or who is King
> God bless us all—that's quite another thing.
>   J. Byrom

You may care to re-write the first two lines, putting in their personal names in place of 'the King' and 'the Pretender'. What people would not have agreed with you in 1745?

1 The Chances of Success in 1745

Imagine a man landing at a lonely spot on the west coast of Scotland in 1745. He has come from France and he has never been in Scotland before. He has only seven other men with him. They treat him as a prince and think of his father as the rightful king of Great Britain and Ireland, even although he is an exile in Italy. He says he has come now in place of his father to win back Great Britain and Ireland, and to give back to his father the crown which is his by right but which he has never worn.

Prince Charles Edward Stuart

The chances had seemed more promising in 1744. With French troops fighting the British army in Europe, Louis XV, the King of France, had been willing to give Charles real help. He had put seven thousand soldiers on board ships at Dunkirk ready to invade Great Britain. Some Highland chiefs would certainly have raised their clans as soon as the French troops landed. But a gale blew, the transport ships were scattered, and the French did not come. This time, in 1745, Prince Charles came by himself, with no French troops and no definite promise of any help from France. On the voyage to Scotland he also lost the ship which was carrying most of the weapons he had bought to arm the Highlanders. As soon as he landed, he sent messages to everyone who might come and support him with armed men.

To rise or not in 1745?

The case for a rising now
Here are some statements Prince Charles made to a Highland chief to prove that the time was ripe for a rising:

Almost all the British troops were abroad. In Scotland there were only a few new raised regiments that had never seen service and could not stand before the Highlanders. The very first advantage gained over the troops would encourage his father's friends at home to declare themselves [for him]. Friends abroad would not fail to give their assistance. He only wanted the Highlanders to start the war.

Home, *History*, 43

1. *What name would describe 'his father's friends at home'?*
2. *Who do you think were his 'friends abroad'?*
3. *What did he expect the Highlanders to do?*
4. *Under the heading 'FOR', on the left hand side of your page, write down as briefly as you can the advantages Charles said they had already (see passage above from Home's History).*

The case against

Lord Elcho, a young man about the same age as Prince Charles, was one of several who had promised to support him if France gave them help:

If the French would give him 6000 men, 30000 louis d'ors [gold pieces] and 10000 stands of arms [sets of weapons] Lord Elcho said he would be joined upon his landing by a great number of his friends, but if he could not obtain these, it was impossible for them to do anything for him.

The Prince said 'he would certainly be in Scotland next summer whether the King of France assisted him or not.' Most of us looked upon it as a mad project and were utterly against it.

Elcho, 234

1. *What three forms of help did Lord Elcho want from the French?*
2. *Could his friends in Scotland do anything for Charles on their own?*
3. *Under the heading 'AGAINST' on the right side of your page, give Elcho's reasons for opposing a rebellion.*
4. *Considering the advice they had given him, was Charles wise or rash to come to Scotland in 1745?*

Lord Elcho did join Prince Charles and served as a cavalry commander.

War, not Peace

When Cameron of Lochiel, the chief of the Cameron clan, met Prince Charles, he advised him to go back to France. Charles refused and said:

'In a few days, with the few friends that I have, I will erect the royal standard, and proclaim to the people of Britain that Charles Stuart is come over to claim the crown of his ancestors, to win it or to perish in the attempt. Lochiel, who, my father has often told me, was our firmest friend, may stay at home, and learn from the newspapers the fate of his prince.'

'No,' said Lochiel, 'I'll share the fate of my prince; and so shall every man over whom nature or fortune have given me power.'

On the result of this conversation depended peace or war. For it is a point agreed among the Highlanders that if Lochiel had persisted in his refusal to take arms, the other Chiefs would not have joined the standard without him.

Home, *History*, 44–5

1. Was Lochiel in favour of a rising at this time?
2. How did Prince Charles succeed in persuading him?
3. Why was Lochiel's support so important to Charles?
4. Group discussion. Imagine you are in a group of Highland chiefs and discuss whether you should raise your clansmen or not.

Prince Charles lands in Scotland. (This engraving was done in the middle of the last century, about one hundred years after Prince Charles landed)

2 Clans and Chiefs

Captain Edward Burt, an Englishman who was in the Highlands with General Wade, discovered much that surprised him in the north. He published *Letters from a Gentleman in the North of Scotland* to explain the Highlands and the Highlanders to English readers:

The Highlanders are divided into Tribes or Clans, under Chiefs; each Clan is again divided into branches from the main stock, who have Chieftains over them. I shall use the word Chief for the Head of the Whole Clan.

The ordinary Highlanders love their Chief and pay him a blind obedience, although it be in opposition to the Government, the laws of the Kingdom, or even the law of God. He is their idol; and as they know no King but him they say they ought to do whatever he commands without enquiry.

Burt, *Letters II*, 105–6

1. What other word does Burt use for a clan?
2. What was the head of a clan called?
3. What was the duty of the clansmen towards him?
4. (a) Who was the chief law-giver for the ordinary Highland clansman?
   (b) If a clan chief rebelled against the King and the government, what would his clansmen be expected to do?

Not every Highlander, however, was prepared to follow his chief without question or murmuring. Usually the further men lived from the chief, the less willing they were to fight for him. Consider the Camerons on the moor of Rannoch, for example, away from the main clan area:

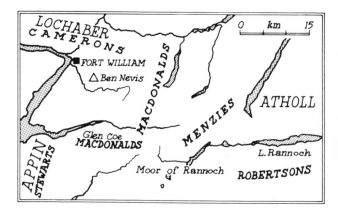

Upon Thursday the 15th August, five heads of the several tribes of the name of Cameron, came from [Cameron of] Lochiel's country and entered Rannoch with a party of their servants and followers to the number of 24. They went from house to house on both sides of Loch Rannoch and intimated to all the Camerons, who were pretty numerous, that if they did not forthwith go along with them, they would that instant proceed to burn all their houses and haugh [*lame or*

cripple] their cattle. Whereupon they carried off about a hundred, mostly of the name of Cameron.

Atholl, vol III, 7

Four days later they were among the 800 Camerons who joined the Jacobite army at Glenfinnan.

1. *How many Camerons came from the moor of Rannoch?*
2. *For what reasons did they come?*

Orders for the march into England from the Clan Appin Order Book

(reprinted by permission of the Scottish United Services Museum)

The clan as a fighting unit

The chief commanded the clan in battle and his close relatives served as officers. When the clan was drawn up,

The front rank was composed of gentlemen who were all provided with targets [*shields*] and were otherwise better armed than the rear. The chief was posted in the centre of the column beside the colours [*clan flag*] and he stood between two brothers, cousins or other relations. The common men were also disposed [*drawn up*] according to their relationship, the father, the son and the brother standing beside each other.

The Stewarts of Appin, 124–5

This is how one clan, the Stewarts of Appin, was made up and arranged for war. The chief himself was a boy, too young to lead the clan. His place was taken by his nearest kinsman, Stewart of Ardsheal. There were four main families or branches, besides the chief's own family and his immediate followers. These were all gentlemen. They were all related to one another and claimed that they and their chief were descended from the same ancestor. Below them in rank were the commoners, their tenants, who stood behind them against the enemy on the battlefield. The list on page 10 shows clearly who the men of Appin were and how many of them were killed or wounded at Culloden:

	Killed	Wounded
Stewart of Ardsheal's family	8	3
Stewart of Fasnacloich's family	2	4
Stewart of Achnacone's family	2	0
Stewart of Invernahyle's family	4	12
Stewarts, followers of Appin	6	6
	22	25

Commoners, followers of Appin

	Killed	Wounded
M'Colls	18	15
Maclarens	13	4
Carmichaels	6	2
M'Combichs	5	3
M'Intyres	5	5
M'Inneses	4	2
MacKenzies	2	3
M'Cormicks (Buchanans)	5	1
M'Lachlans	2	0
Macleas or Livingstones	4	1
Others	6	4
Total of killed and wounded	92	65

The Stewarts of Appin, 124

1 (a) Who was usually the military leader of a clan?
(b) Who led the Stewarts in the 'Forty-five'?

2. Clans contained both gentlemen and commoners. What were the differences between them:
(a) in rank
(b) in the weapons they carried
(c) in their position on the field of battle?

3. (a) What do you notice about the surnames of the commoners, considering the clan they were in?
(b) Suggest a phrase to describe all these men which is more accurate than 'The Stewarts of Appin'?
(b) Is the following statement TRUE or UNTRUE?—'A Highland clan is a set of men bearing the same surname.'

4. Add together the totals of those killed and those wounded in this clan at Culloden. Assuming that the Stewarts of Appin numbered 300 at Culloden, rewrite and complete the following sentence:
. . . out of 300 of the Stewarts of Appin were killed or wounded at the Battle of Culloden—roughly, one out of every . . . .

How many men might join?

	I.	2.
Fighting men in the Highlands in 1724		*Clans on Jacobite side in 1746*

Clans	Number of men	
Campbells	5 000	
MacKenzies	2 000	
Grants	850	
Camerons	800	Camerons
Mackintoshes	800	Mackintoshes
MacDonalds of Sleat	700	
MacDonalds of Clanranald	700	MacDonalds of Clanranald
MacLeods	700	
Frasers	900	Frasers
MacLeans	500	MacLeans
MacDonalds of Glengarry	500	MacDonalds of Glengarry
MacGregors	700	MacGregors
Farquharsons	500	Farquharsons
MacKays	800	
Stewarts of Appin	300	Stewarts of Appin
Macphersons	400	Macphersons
Munros	350	
Rosses	500	
MacLachlans	200	MacLachlans
McDougalls	200	
McKinnons	200	
Robertsons	200	Robertsons
Chisholms	200	Chisholms
MacDonalds of Keppoch	150	MacDonalds of Keppoch
MacDonalds of Glencoe	130	MacDonalds of Glencoe
Grants of Glenmoriston	150	Grants of Glenmoriston

Manners of the Highlanders, 1, 26

3 Who became Jacobites?

How much do we know about each of the men who followed Prince Charles? Do we know their names, their occupations, where they came from, what happened to them? We do not know all of them; but we know something about a lot of them and a lot about some of them.

There could have been as many as 10 000 men altogether who served the Jacobite cause at some time between August 1745 and April 1746. We have two main sources of information about them:

1. *A List of Persons concerned in the Rebellion 1745–46*
2. *The Prisoners of the '45*, in three volumes.

These were published by the Scottish History Society and there will probably be copies in your local library. In the *List* are some two and a half thousand names. It was made up by local tax-collectors after the rebellion. It is probably fairly complete on the Jacobites who came from Lowland areas, but does not record the names of nearly all the Highland clansmen who took part. We can prove this by comparing surnames in the *List* and in *Prisoners of the '45*. For example, the *List* names 32 Mackenzies who took part in the rising: *Prisoners of the '45* contains 112 of that

name who were taken prisoner! Again, the *List* contains the names of only two Chisholms but one of them, Roderick Chisholm, son of the chief, is described as having 'headed about eighty of the Chisholms at the Battle of Culloden, himself and 30 whereof were killed'. Taken together the *List* and *Prisoners of the '45* tell us the names and some facts about 6 000 of the men who followed Prince Charles. The men we know nothing about are likely to have been Highlanders, particularly those who were killed or who escaped being taken prisoner.

Occupations

What had been the occupations of those named in the *List* who joined the Jacobite army? Landowners were the biggest group, followed by servants, then farmers, and so on as in the list below:

Landowners
Servants
Farmers
Labourers
Merchants
Workmen
Brewers
Shoemakers
Lawyers.

Besides these, there were men from an astonishing variety of jobs: butchers, bakers and a candle-maker, carters and miners, blacksmiths and gunsmiths, pipers and fiddlers, besides a beggar and a dancing-master, a gaoler and a snuff-grinder. There were also four schoolmasters, two schoolboys and five others, simply described as 'boys'.

1. *What are the jobs of the men on the right?*
2. *Write down the occupations in the list on page 12 which you connect with the land.*
3. *Which occupations do you connect more with the town than the country?*

The next two pages give the names of some of these people from different parts of the country, with notes on what they did and what happened to them.

Perhaps one of the men named came from near where you live. If not, there are another two and half thousand in the *List*!

Only about 300 of them were said to be prisoners. The other source we have, *The Prisoners of the '45*, contains the names of three and a half thousand people, all of whom had been taken prisoner. Of these, over a third were set free, whereas nearly a thousand were transported to become slaves in British colonies in America or the West Indies, two hundred were banished from Britain, 120 were executed and the rest must have died from their wounds or from fever in prison.

Some of the occupations followed by Lowlanders who became Jacobites (reconstruction)

WHO	WHAT	WHERE FROM	CHARGE AGAINST HIM	FATE
From Aberdeen and round about				
Robert Ewing	Soldier and deserter	Charlestown	Carried arms at Falkirk and Culloden	Killed
Robert Findlay	Labouring servant	Balfidie	Carried arms at Culloden but said to be forced	Not known
George Law	Minister	Aberdeen	Carried arms with the rebels, was at Stirling siege and Culloden (Chaplain to rebels, with them to Derby and back, not seen carrying weapons)	Set free
William Law, George Law's son	14–15 year-old schoolboy	Aberdeen	Carried arms, seen with small sword and white cockade	Set free
From Dundee and district				
Thomas Crighton	Surgeon	Dundee	Acted as surgeon, joined after Prestonpans and carried arms with rebels till after Culloden	Near Blairgowrie lurking
John Edward	Tenant	Needs	Pressed to carry arms with the rebels, deserted them at Carlisle and would not join again though they kindled a fire to burn his house	At home
Andrew Laird	Merchant	Dundee	Aided rebels, opened post-bag, letters, etc.	In Dundee Prison
William Thomson	Workman	Little Kenny	Served as volunteer with rebels	Captured at Carlisle, transported to Leeward Islands
From Edinburgh				
John Finlayson	Mathematical instrument-maker	Edinburgh	Worked with rebel artillery	Prisoner after Culloden, taken to London but set free in 1747
John Goodwillie	Lawyer	Edinburgh	Wore tartans and a white cockade; helped to raise money, etc.	Not known
Marmaduke McBeath	Powder-flask maker	Canongate	One of rebel cavalry, raised money for them; with them at all the battles to the end	About Edinburgh lurking
Walter Orrock	Shoemaker, Deacon of Shoemakers and Town Councillor	Edinburgh	The day of Prestonpans Battle came riding furiously up the Canongate with a white cockade, crying, 'Victory, victory, the Prince has won the day,' and shut the Netherbow Port against the fleeing soldiers, several of whom fell into rebel hands	Near Leven in Fife

From near Inverness

Simon Fraser, Lord Lovat	Head of Fraser clan	Castle Downie	Raised his clan on the rebel side; tried for high treason	Beheaded
Simon Fraser	Tenant	Beauly	Soldier in rebel service	Killed at Culloden
Donald Fraser	Blacksmith	Moy	Captain in rebel army, promoted on account of great services [see Rout of Moy p.20]	Skulking
Alastair McGillivray	[Laird] of Dunmaglass		Colonel in said army and very active, said to be forced out by Lady Anne McIntosh	Killed at Culloden

From Glasgow
People in Glasgow were not in sympathy with the Jacobites and very few helped them. Here are some who did:

Peter Bell	—	Glasgow	Joined rebel Life Guards at Glasgow on their retreat. Influenced by his mother	Not known
Thomas Robertson	Barber	Gorbals	Enlisted in rebel army and continued to the end	Not known
James Stirling of Keir	Landowner	Calder	Influenced his two sons to join Prince Charles; helped Jacobites in Glasgow	Prisoner in Dumbarton Castle, made get-away on Dutch ship, but recaptured. Released 1747
Andrew Wood	Shoemaker	Glasgow	Captain in rebel army at Culloden	Taken prisoner, executed in London

Details about some of the men who followed Prince Charles
(taken from *A List of Persons concerned in the Rebellion 1745–6*)

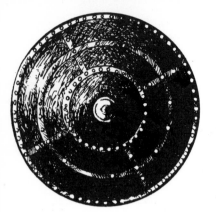

4 Arms and Supplies for the Highland Army

It was impossible to provide the new army with all the supplies and good weapons they needed at once. Chiefs and clansmen brought what they could but they could not be expected to provide all that they needed by themselves. Weapons had become scarce since the Disarming Act of 1716. Prince Charles brought some, but few of good quality — 'about 1600 bad guns and as many worse swords,' the government were told. Because there weren't enough weapons for everyone, some men had to be sent home.

Weapons

What did they need?
The weapons used by the Highlanders and their methods of fighting with them were clearly described by General Wade and his assistant, Edward Burt:

The arms they make use of in war are a musket, a broadsword and a target, a pistol and a dirk or

Target or targe; Powder horn;
Dirk; Broadsword (reconstruction)

dagger, with a powder horn and a pouch for their ammunition. When in sight of the enemy they endeavour to possess themselves of the highest ground, believing they descend on them with greater force. After their first fire (they rarely stand a second), they throw away their firearms and plaids which encumber them and make their attack with their swords. If repulsed, they seldom or never rally.

Burt, *Letters II*, 220–222

1. According to the above list, how many separate pieces of equipment did each clansman need?
2. If he could not have them all, which would he particularly want? Make a list starting with the most important and finishing with the least important, in your opinion. Think of what was liable to be used most, and remember that they had all to be carried.
3. Why did the Highlanders try to occupy the highest ground?

What did they have?
Here is a description in verse of the Highland army and its equipment. It is by Dougal Graham, a deformed pedlar, who became a camp-follower of the Jacobites from Stirling onwards and later wrote his *History of the Rebellion*, more than a hundred pages of verse which he sold for four pence a copy. Of the first clans to join Prince Charles he said they:

Numbered one thousand eight hundred men,
But badly armed, as you may ken;
With *lockless* guns and rusty swords   [*without the firing mechanism*]
Dirks and pistols of ancient sorts
Old scythes, *with their rumples even*   [*even bent ones*]
Into a tree they had them driven
And some with batons of good oak
Vowed to kill at every stroke:
Some had hatchets upon a pole
Mischievous weapons, *antique and droll*   [*old and funny*]
Graham, History, 87

Pistol; Musket (reconstruction)

How did they get what they needed?
Prince Charles' secretary thought that the
scarcity of swords and shields, called targets
or targes, was the most serious. Before the
rising he was coolly ordering weapons in
Edinburgh. Once it began he sent men to get
arms and ammunition wherever they could:

Finding an armourer in Edinburgh had got
between three and four hundred blades, I
bargained with him to mount them [*put handles
on them*] at half a guinea. I did not get the whole
[of them], yet the rest came in good time. I
employed a gunsmith to pick up all the muskets
he could find. I likewise ordered a number of
targets at Edinburgh which were made, and
brought to the army the night before the battle of
Prestonpans.

Murray of Broughton, 132

**Other ways of arming the Highlanders are
revealed in this letter from Lord George**

Murray, the Jacobite General, to his brother,
the Duke of Atholl:

24th Sept.

Dear Brother,
    We have 1 000 stand of arms more than we
want at present. 2 000 targes and 500 tents are
furnished by the Town of Edinburgh. With what
we got from Cope's army, they will serve nearly
double our number,
I am,
Yours,
George Murray.
W. Duke, *Lord George Murray and the Forty-five*, 88

1. (a) What did Dougal Graham say was wrong
with their (i) guns, (ii) swords, (iii) pistols?
(b) Do you think the Highland army with the
weapons Dougal Graham described would have
frightened the soldiers of the British army?
(c) How were they able to get weapons from
General Cope's army? (See page 27.)
2. What is: a targe, a musket, an armourer?

Food

If you have ever been on a camping holiday, you will know how much time and effort it takes to get the food you need, to carry it with you and to cook it to keep you going until the next day. You can imagine how much more difficult it was to feed a new army on the move when its numbers had risen to nearly two thousand men. Lord George Murray tried to see that they all had enough food to start with, and something to carry it in, before they left Perth for the south. As he wrote to his brother, the Duke of Atholl:

> Perth, 7 Sept
>
> Dear Bro,
>
> I hope the oatmeal was with you this day, 35 bolls.* I shall have more meal with you on Monday night for you must distribute a peck† a man, and cost what it will, there must be pokes [*simple bags or pouches*] made to contain a peck or two, for the men to have always with them. Buy linen, harn [*sackcloth*] or anything for these pokes are of absolute necessity.
>
> Yours,
>
> George Murray.
>
> Saturday, nine at night
>
> Murray, *Marches*, 31

Murray's men made over a thousand of these pokes for the army, and after filling them with oatmeal and 'as many threepenny loaves as would be three days' bread,' they set off from Perth. Bread and cheese were their usual fare at midday when they were on the march. Men who are hungry on the march will steal, as Dougal Graham tells us below. Thieves were severely punished and everyone was told to pay for the food he needed:

> Many of his crew indeed were greedy
> To fill their bellies when they were needy
> They cocks and hens, and churns and cheese
> Did kill and eat, when they could seize.
>
> Graham, *History*, 90

1. What was the basic food of the Highland army?
2. Who carried it?
3. What would happen if they did not have enough?

*a boll: a grain measure, equal to 140 lbs (64 kg).
†a peck: about 9 lbs or 4 kg.

Dress

The men in the Highland army were dressed in tartan. The chiefs saw it as their duty to provide the clothes that their men needed to start with. When these were worn out, towns on the way found that they were expected to replace them. Here is how Edmund Burt described the dress of the Highlanders:

Gentlemen wear trews, that is, the breeches and stockings all of one piece and drawn on together. Over this they wear a plaid, which is usually three yards long and two breadths wide. The whole garb is made of chequered tartan.

With the ordinary Highlander a small part of the plaid is set in folds and girt round the waist to make of it a short petticoat or kilt, that reaches half way down the thigh, and the rest is brought over the shoulders, and then fastened, often with a fork, and sometimes with a bodkin [*a pin*] or a sharpened piece of stick. The plaid serves for a cloak by day and bedding at night. It makes them ready at a moment's warning to join in any rebellion as they continually carry their tents about them.

Burt, *Letters*, 186–90

Lord George Murray
(*from the Duke of Atholl's collection at Blair Castle*)

5 Women and the Jacobites

Was it only men who came to the aid of Prince Charles? The two sources which follow show that many women in Edinburgh voiced their support and some hurried to pay their respects to him at Holyrood Palace:

At the Cross when the Heralds proclaimed King James, 'the populace huzzaed [*cheered*]. A number of the ladies in the windows strained their voices with acclamation [*shouts of applause*], and their arms with waving white handkerchiefs in honour of the day. These demonstrations of joy were chiefly confined to one sex: few gentlemen were to be seen on the streets or in the windows.'

Home, *History*, 102

That night to Holyrood 'came a great many ladies of fashion to kiss his hand, but his behaviour to them was very cool. He had not been much used to women's company, and was always embarrassed when he was with them.'

Elcho, 259

1. Who strained their voices and their arms?
2. Who did not?
3. Why do you think the handkerchiefs they waved were white ones?
4. How did Charles behave towards the ladies of fashion?
5. What would they think of him a month later?

The applause of these ladies was of no practical use to his cause. In the north, Lady Anne Mackintosh did far more to help him. Her husband, the chief of the clan Mackintosh, was a captain on the government side. In spite of what his wishes would have been, she raised the men of the clan herself, as if she were the clan chief. She did not lead them in battle (see chapter 3 for Alastair McGillivray who did) but she is often called 'Colonel Anne'.

On the way north in February, 1746, Prince Charles was almost captured at her home at Moy by a large government force. The blacksmith, called Donald Fraser (see chapter 3, p.15), and a handful of men saved him. Walking up and down shouting and firing off their muskets in the dark they made the enemy think there were hundreds of Jacobite troops present. The government force made off in a hurry towards Inverness. This little incident is called 'the Rout of Moy'. Two months later, she was expecting another victory at Culloden. Instead, Mackintosh women were wailing for their men who lay dead or were wounded there. Lady Anne Mackintosh and three other titled ladies were taken prisoner but were soon set free:

The ladies, after tea, were preparing to dress for a ball in the evening, expecting the rebels had gained the victory, but the King's Redcoats were so rude as to interrupt them, and lead them up a dance they did not expect. The rebels had ordered all the inhabitants of Inverness to provide all the oatmeal they could spare, and with it bake bannocks for their suppers, against their return from the victory; but their disappointment was very pleasing to us, who came to eat it in their stead.

Ray, *Complete History*, 343

1. *How did Lady Anne Mackintosh help Prince Charles?*
2. *How did Donald Fraser help Prince Charles?*
3. *In the last extract,*
   (a) how did these ladies intend to celebrate the victory?
   (b) how did the rebel soldiers hope to celebrate the victory?
   (c) on whose side was the person who wrote the passage and how do you know?

Flora MacDonald is by far the most famous woman in the events of 1745–46. She was not involved in the rising at all, only in helping Prince Charles when he was on the run after it was all over. She was then 24, the daughter of a South Uist farmer. She managed to get him past the men who were hunting for him, by passing him off as an Irish servant, a good spinner called Betty Burke. He (or she) was dressed in a flowered linen dress with a white apron and cap. Several people thought her an odd-looking servant: she took such long strides in walking, for instance. Five

Flora MacDonald

MacDonalds rowed them across the stormy sea to Skye during the night. The Prince was never captured: Flora MacDonald soon was. She was taken as a prisoner to London where she was allowed a good deal of freedom and was never brought to trial. She was in the company of Prince Charles for only four days but what she did to save him has secured her place in history.

1. *Why did the government want to capture Prince Charles?*
2. *How did Flora MacDonald help him?*
3. *Where did she take him?*
4. *Why was she arrested?*
5. *Why do you think she was not tried?*

Did you know that there were some women with the Jacobite army? There were also some who attached themselves to the British army. Commanders did not like to have their troops on the march slowed down by having a long 'tail' of women and children tagging along behind them. They tried to stop them by not giving their soldiers permission to marry but many of the women still followed the regiment and were known as 'regimental women'.

When the Jacobite army left Edinburgh on 1st November to invade England, this order was given:

The Colonels and other Officers are forbid to suffer any woman to follow their Regiment, but [*except*] the women they really know to be married.

Appin Order Book

The Jacobite camp at Duddingston (detail)

1. Who were allowed to follow the Jacobite army?
2. Who were not?

Many seem to have gone just the same, since more than fifty 'regimental women' were captured during the retreat north towards Scotland. They may have found the pace of the march too much for them, or they may have been too frightened to wade across the River Esk, which was in flood. Or they may have stayed behind to nurse soldiers who were sick or wounded. We do not know. Half the women prisoners, like so many of the men, were transported to the West Indies, where they had to work in the sugar plantations. One of them, Jane Herring, from East Lothian, had been a washerwoman; another, Mary Kennedy, whose ten year old son, Angus, was transported along with her, had done sewing and washing for men in a regiment of MacDonalds.

Three of the women captured near Carlisle were Ann Layread who came from Inverness, Margaret Straughson from Aberdeen, and Jane Mathewson, whose birthplace is not known. They were put in prison at Whitehaven, a port on the coast of Cumberland which dealt in sugar and rum from the West Indies. Eight months later they were busy trying to get out. They succeeded in digging a tunnel right under the prison wall, and crawled through it to the world outside and to freedom.

6 The Highlanders in Edinburgh

In Edinburgh people did not believe that their city would fall to the Highland army. Even when the enemy was near they still felt quite safe. On Monday, September 16, the *Caledonian Mercury* brought them the latest news:

Yesterday morning we were assured that the Highlanders were arrived at Linlithgow, 12 miles west of here. At eleven o'clock the fire bell of this city was rung in order to alarm and arm the inhabitants. We were very quiet all night and now expect a visit. The whole city is in arms and ready to give them a warm reception.

1. *If you had been an Edinburgh citizen reading this, which items in it might have made you worry?*
2. *What information in it would have made you feel more confident?*

The following day, the same paper announced:

Affairs in this city have taken the most surprising turn since yesterday, without the least bloodshed or opposition, so that we now have in our streets Highlanders and Bagpipes in place of Dragoons and Drums.

1. *Who were now in control of the city?*
2. *Was the writer surprised, and why?*
3. *Would you have been?*

How did the Highlanders capture the city without any fighting?

After two in the morning, Prince Charles ordered Cameron of Lochiel to put his people under arms and Mr. Murray to be their guide. He gave strict orders to behave with all moderation to the inhabitants, that the sogers should not be allowed to taste spirits, and to pay for whatever they got. He promised them two shillings [*10p*] each as soon as they [were] masters of the place. They arrived at the Netherbow Port [the east gate of the town], without meeting anybody on the way.

It was now clear daylight. A coach came down the High Street and obliged the Guard to open the Port [*gate*]. Lochiel rushed in, the guard immediately dispersing.

800 Highlanders followed him in, and the city was theirs, with no shots being fired and no blood spilt.

Murray of Broughton, 194

1. *Why do you think Lochiel's men were 'not allowed to taste spirits'?*
2. *At two shillings per man, how much would the capture of Edinburgh have cost the Prince?*
3. *(a) At what time of day did the Highlanders capture the city?*
   (b) Where were most of the inhabitants then?

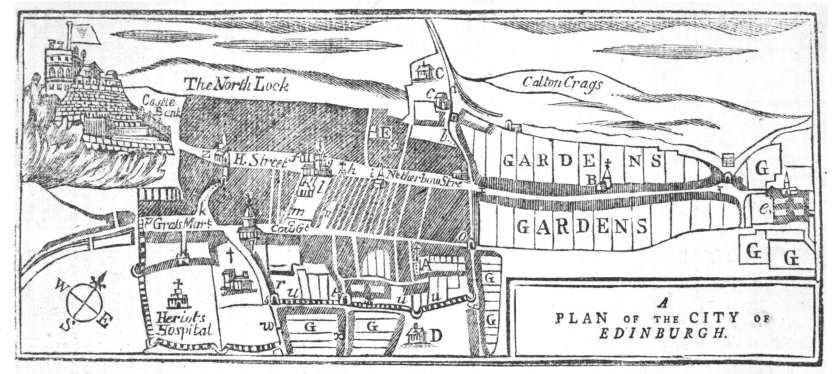

The North Lock

Calton Crags

Castle Bank

GARDENS

GARDENS

H. Street

Netherbow Stre

GreisMart

Cowgt

G

G

Heriots Hospital

G

G

G

D

A
PLAN OF THE CITY OF
EDINBURGH.

Paſſages from the High-ſtreet North. 1ſt, Fleſhmarket cloſs. 2d, Hackerſton's wynd. 3d, Lieth wynd. *Paſſages down from* High-ſtreet *to the* Cowgait *reckon'd from* k *the* Weſt Bow *Eaſtward.* 1ſt, Liberton's wynd. 2d, Foſter's wynd. 3d, Beſs wynd. 4 Kirk heugh. 5 St Mannan's wynd. 6 Fiſh-market, with 2 paſſages into it. 7 Borths wick's cloſs. 8 Cow cloſs. 9 Bells wynd. 10 Stephen Law's cloſs. 11 Peebles wynd. 12 Marlin's wynd. 13 Nidderies wynd. 14 Dickſon's cloſs. 15 Black Fryar wynd. 16 Tedrick's wynd. 17 Gray's cloſs. 18 St Mary's wynd. *c* College kirk. *d* The Calton. *e* Holy Rood Houſe. *f* Talbooth. *g* StGiles's. *b* The Croſs. *i* Tron kirk, at the back of which is the poultry market. *k* Weſt Bow. *l* Parliament houſe. *m* Meal-market. *n* Fiſh market. *O* Cowgate port. *p* Weſt port. *q* Magdalen chappel. *r* The Society. *s* Society port. *t* Potter Row port. *u. u. u.* Town wall. *w* Society ſuburbs. *x* Potter's Row ſuburbs. *y* The Pleaſants. *z* Weighouſe. *Note,* TheWeſt kirk lies behind the caſtle, and therefore does not appear in this plan. A.Lady Yeſter's kirk. B The Cannon Gate kirk. C The Orphan hoſpital. D The Infirmary. E The Fleſh market. G G G Gardens; ‡‡ Street call'd Canongait.† Grey Fryers Kirk. (*See p.* 529.)

Edinburgh in 1745
(from *The Gentleman's Magazine*)

The Arrival of the Prince

John Home, who was to write a history of 'the '45', stood in the crowd:

About ten o'clock the main body of the rebels marching by Duddingston entered the King's Park and halted under the peak called Arthur's Seat. By and by Charles came, accompanied by the Highland Chiefs and other commanders of his army.

The Park was full of people, all impatient to see this extraordinary person. He was in the prime of youth, tall and handsome, of a fair complexion.

He had a light coloured wig with his own hair combed over the front. He wore the Highland dress, that is a tartan short coat without the plaid, a blue bonnet on his head, and on his breast the star of the order of St. Andrew. Charles stood some time in the Park to show himself to the people. Then, though he was very near the palace [Holyrood] he mounted his horse, either to [be seen better] or because he rode well, and looked graceful on horseback. . . .

Home, *History*, 99–100

1. Make a list of the words and phrases John Home uses in praise of the Prince. (Home later fought against the Highlanders.)
2. Find the Netherbow Port and Holyrood on the map on page 24.
3. See also chapter 5, page 20, for the way Edinburgh people cheered him. Do you think they would have done so, if the Highlanders had had to fight fiercely to capture the city?

At noon the Highland army and a great crowd of people assembled at the Cross in the High Street. They heard the Heralds proclaim James VIII King and Prince Charles sole regent with power to act for him. Prince Charles now occupied Holyrood Palace, the Highland army was in camp nearby at Duddingston and Highlanders stood guard at important points in the town. Edinburgh was in their hands and, to everyone's surprise, the British army under Sir John Cope was unable to take it from them. (See next chapter.)

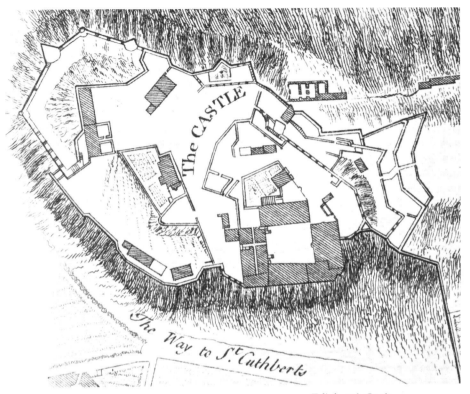

Edinburgh Castle
(detail from plan of city and castle of Edinburgh drawn by W. Edgar in 1765)

The Jacobites and the Castle

Soldiers in the Castle were able to hold it, in spite of attempts by the Highlanders to dislodge them. One of these attacks was described in the *Edinburgh Evening Courant* on October 5 as follows:

The garrison [*soldiers defending it*] in the Castle set the ruinous house, on the north side of the Castle Hill, on fire, together with the old foundry, which burned with great violence. In the meantime, the cannons played [*fired*] and the garrison made a sally [*rushed out to attack*]. What loss the Highlanders or the garrison sustained is not known.

Equipment and More Men

Charles now wanted to build up his army and expected Edinburgh to equip it.

The 18th September in the morning the Prince sent Lord Elcho to the Magistrates to demand 1 000 tents, 2 000 targets, 6 000 pairs of shoes and 6 000 water cantines. The Magistrates agreed to it, and the workmen were set immediately to work. . . . The tents, targets, cantines etc., ordered from ye town of Edinburgh were delivered and distributed to the men at Duddingston.

Elcho, 262, 282

1. Did Edinburgh supply all that was asked for?
2. How many men did Prince Charles expect to have?

According to John Home, there were nearly as many as that before they left Edinburgh:

They exceeded 5 500, of whom 400 or 500 were cavalry. Of the whole number, not quite 4 000 were real Highlanders who formed the Clan regiments, and were indeed the strength of the rebel army. All the regiments of foot wore Highland garb [*dress*]. The pay of a Captain in this army was half a crown [*two shillings and sixpence*] a day; the pay of a lieutenant two shillings; the pay of an ensign [*an officer of the lowest rank*], one shilling and sixpence; and every private man received sixpence a day, without deduction. The front rank of each regiment consisted of persons who called themselves gentlemen, and were paid one shilling a day.

Home, *History*, 137

A shilling contained 12 pennies, 12d. It became 5p when our present coins came into use. To tell how much a soldier's pay was worth then, however, we need to know how high prices were. Here are some prices paid for food in or near Edinburgh in 1745, taken from Prince Charles' own Household Book:

Beef 2d–2½d per lb
Cheese 4d per lb
Butter 7d–8d per lb
Eggs 3½d per dozen
Pears 3d per dozen
Chickens 4½d each
Hens or ducks 8d–10d each
A sheep 6/–.

Lyon in Mourning, vol 2, 115–52

7 The Battle of Prestonpans

By marching his army to Fort George in the north, General Sir John Cope missed the Jacobite army in the Highlands. Instead, he allowed them to enter the Lowlands without opposition and, as we have seen, to capture the capital without bloodshed. With all haste, he brought his men south and they arrived at Dunbar by sea. They marched towards Edinburgh.

Hearing that he was on his way, the Highlanders set out from Edinburgh to fight him. They met on a stretch of bare low land, chosen by Cope, near Prestonpans and the sea.

(It is suggested that you now tackle Workguide 7, numbers 1–3.)

The Jacobite commander, Lord George Murray, decided that a direct attack from Tranent would be too risky. If only they could get round the ditches in front of them, without being seen, they could take the enemy by surprise. The ground to the east was marshy, but there was a track through it and a local man, Robert Anderson, guided them, as they moved silently under cover of darkness. All went well until a patrol of cavalry became suspicious and raised the alarm. Cope's men had spent the night drawn up for battle. Suddenly they had all to turn to face an attack from the one front on which they had no protection, the east.

Just as the sun rose, the whole Highland army appeared. First Cope's gunners and then his cavalry fled. Here is the short report the *Edinburgh Evening Courant* gave of this brief battle:

The onset was given with the greatest courage that was ever perhaps known. The Highlanders bore down all before them. The dispute was short, few discharges [of muskets] made, the broadsword did all. In a few minutes, General Cope's army was totally routed, and the baggage taken. Many were killed and more prisoners. General Cope escaped, as we hear, to Berwick.

Routes followed by the Jacobites and the British Army under General Cope before the Battle of Prestonpans

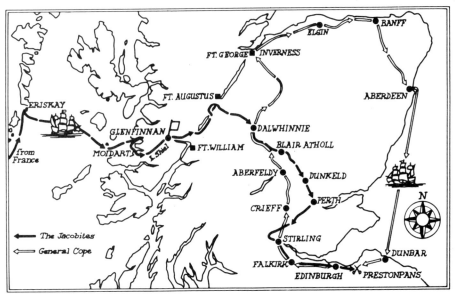

8 The Highland Army in England

In the weeks that followed their victory at Prestonpans the Highland officers looked for signs that France would now send troops or that people in England would rally to fight for Prince Charles. When nothing at all happened to encourage them they were not willing to invade England. The Prince said to them, 'I find, Gentlemen, you are for staying in Scotland, and defending your country, and I am resolved to go to England.'

1. Who were the new masters of Scotland after the battle of Prestonpans?
2. Who had become the ruler of Scotland in fact?
3. For what reasons did the chiefs want to stay and hold Scotland?
4. Why did Prince Charles want them to march into England?

He had his way. The Highland army marched south and crossed the Border into the northwest of England where they captured Carlisle, but there is evidence that many of the men were very unhappy about going out of Scotland. Hundreds deserted, that is, they left the army without permission. Lord Elcho, who rode with the cavalry, tells us how many: The army at leaving Edinburgh was 5 500 and at Carlisle only 4 500.

The *Evening Courant* of November 8 had news of some of them:

Deserters swarm daily from the Highland army. We hear for their encouragement, that General Blakeney the Governor of Stirling Castle has opened the Pass at Stirling, and allows them to go unmolested [*without being harmed*], on laying down their Arms.

1. How do you think the Highland soldiers felt about going to England?
2. How many Highlanders deserted between Edinburgh and Carlisle?
3. Where did they go?
4. On what condition were they allowed to pass through Stirling?

What did the English think of the invaders?

The people of England did not welcome the Highlanders, and were happy to see them move on out of their district. The Highlanders needed to be fed after a long day's march and expected the local people to cook for them. Their horsemen became unpopular because they rode about the countryside looking for fresh horses for themselves to ride or to pull their baggage waggons. Here is how one man, the postmaster in Penrith in Cumberland described these strangers in their midst:

They march with droves of black cattle and sheep, waggons of biscake and cheese, which they sit down at noon to eat. At night and morning they get a little oatmeal which they buy up at their own price or take away whenever they can get it, and constantly carry it in a leather bag at their side. . . . They march always by day break and sooner when they have the benefit of the moon. The main body encamps [*pitches tents*] every night: the officers go to the towns or houses.

State Papers T3/93
Jarvis, *Collected Papers*, Vol. II, 64

1. Make a list of the facts you had learned already which the postmaster mentions about the food or equipment of the Highland army.
2. Why do you think they had cattle and sheep with them — to sell or to eat?
3. What two complaints were made against the Highlanders, and which is worse?
4. When did the Highlanders march off each day?

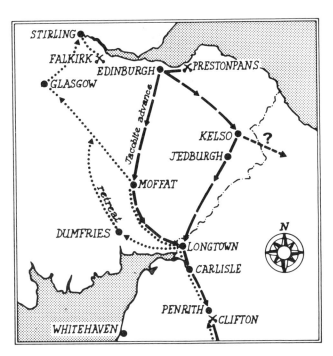

Routes followed by the Jacobites on their journey to and from Derby (northern map)

Penrith is only thirty miles into England. The people of that place could have been watching the new masters of Britain pass by. But as the Highlanders moved further and further south where none of them except the few who had been cattle drovers had ever been before, their chances of success seemed to be fading away. Almost no one at all in England was prepared to join them and fight for their Prince. The November days and nights were growing cold, were closing in around them now outnumbered them by six to one. When they reached Derby on December 4 Prince Charles, ever hopeful, might point out that it was only another 130 miles to London. Looking the other way, it was nearly 200 miles back to the nearest part of Scotland.

1. Did the Highlanders win many recruits in the north of England?
2. Where was the British army by early December?

Here is a good description of the state of the Highland army on the day it arrived in Derby.

The whole vanguard [*men at the front of the army*] came in, consisting of about 30 men. They wore goldlaced hats with white cockades. They were clothed in blue faced with red, had on scarlet waistcoats trimmed with gold lace, and most of them being likely young men, made a handsome appearance. They sat on horseback in the market-place near three hours. They ordered the bells to be rung and bonfires to be made, which was done accordingly.

Then Lord Elcho with the Life-Guards and many of the Chiefs also arrived on horseback, to the number of about 150, most of them clothed as above. These made a fine show, being the flower of their army.

Soon after, their main body marched into town, six or eight abreast, with about eight standards, most of which were white flags with a red cross. They had several bag-pipers who played as they marched along. They were in general a crew of shabby, lousy, pitiful-look'd fellows, mixed up with old men and boys, dressed in dirty plaids and as dirty shoes, without breeches. They wore their stockings made of plaid, not much above half way up their legs, some without shoes or next to none, and with their plaids thrown over their shoulders, they appeared more like a parcel of chimney-sweepers than soldiers.

We were obliged to treat them as we would have done our best friends and set before them bread, cheese, beer and ale, whilst every family were employed in providing hot suppers, and preparing convenient places to lodge them in, some being content to lie on straw and others insisted on beds. Great numbers were not able to speak a word of English but talked a language called Earsh or Wild Irish

Allardyce, *Papers*, vol. II, 287–9

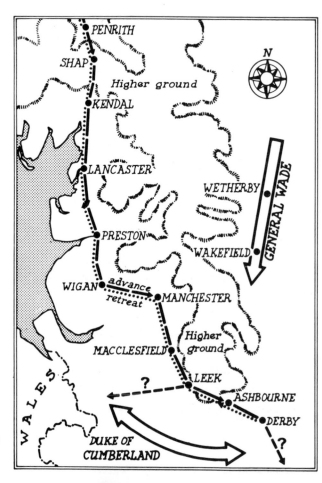

Routes followed by the Jacobites on their journey to and from Derby (southern map)

9 The Return to Scotland

When most of the officers were at the Prince's quarters in Derby, every other officer [except the Duke of Perth], declared their opinions for a retreat. I offered to make the retreat and always to be in the rear myself, and that each regiment would take it in turns [to be the rear-guard] till we came to Carlisle. As all the officers agreed in this opinion, his Royal Highness said he would consent to it, though it was observed he was much disappointed to be so near London, and yet not in a condition to march forwards.

> Murray, *Marches*, 54–6

1. Who had wanted to push on towards London?
2. Who offered to cover the retreat?
3. Why was the Prince 'much disappointed'?

If they were turning for home, they must try to get as far ahead as possible before the Duke of Cumberland's soldiers knew what they were up to. They set off just as it was growing dark, horses at the trot, the clansmen running.

Coming back from Derby

On	Arrived at	Travelled
Dec. 6	Ashbourne	14 miles *
7	Leek	15 miles
8	Macclesfield	13 miles
9	Manchester	18 miles
10	Wigan	19 miles
11	Preston	17 miles —rested
13	Lancaster	22 miles —halted
15	Kendal	22 miles
16	Shap	16 miles
17	Penrith	10 miles —fought off pursuers at Clifton on 18th
19	Carlisle	18 miles
20	Over the Border	11 miles

Rewrite and complete the following sentences:

1. The Highlanders had marched .... miles from Derby to Preston before they had their first day's rest.
2. They had been on the road for .... days before Cumberland's cavalry caught up with them at Clifton.
3. On their retreat from Derby to the Border, the Jacobite army marched .... miles in .... days, an average of .... miles per day.

* Remember, I mile is just over 1½ kilometres.

To bring the Highlanders out of the heart of England with the loss of so very few men was a great achievement, much greater than winning a walking race. Not only did the Duke of Cumberland's army fail to overtake them, General Wade's army based on Newcastle did not arrive in time to cut their line of retreat.

Probably the worst part of the journey was when the waggons stuck on the rough and steep road over Shap Fell, north of Kendal. Here is how Lord George Murray, commanding the rearguard, remembered it:

It proved a very bad, rainy day. By the time I got amongst the hills, I was stopped because the [four-wheeled] waggons could not be carried through a water [*a river or stream*] where there was a narrow turn and a steep ascent [*a slope upwards*]. The horses of two waggons were yoked to one, besides at least forty hands. I was detained there all night. I bought all the oat meal, cheese and other things in the place and distributed it among the men.

As soon as day began to break, we got all the small [two-wheeled] carts that had timber wheels or wheels of one piece of wood we could purchase. We unloaded the waggons and put the things into those small carts. The hill was the steepest and longest on the whole road. I got the men to carry to Shap a good many cannon balls, which eased the carriages much. I gave sixpence [$2\frac{1}{2}p$] the piece for doing it, by which means I got above two hundred carried. It was late before we got to Shap, and here I found most of the cannon, with what ammunition had come along with them.

Murray, *Marches*, 62–5

1. *What had happened to the four-wheeled waggons?*
2. *What did Lord George Murray's men try to do about them at first?*
3. (a) *Why were small carts much better?*
   (b) *What did the men do with the loads in the waggons?*
4. (a) *Why did Lord George Murray not leave the cannon balls behind?*
   (b) *What did a soldier get if he carried one over Shap?*

On December 20 the army waded across the River Esk, the last barrier between them and Scotland. Here is Lord George Murray's account of it.

We were a hundred men abreast, and it was a very fine show. The water was big and took most of them breast-high. I believe there were two thousand men in the water at once. There was no danger. The ford was good and Highlanders will often pass a water [*cross a river*] where horses will not. The pipes began to play so soon as we passed and the men all danced reels, which in a moment dried them.

Murray, *Marches*, 74–5

1. *How would you feel about wading across a river in flood in December?*

2. Why do you think the Highlanders danced reels after crossing?

The Highlanders in Glasgow

Dougal Graham, whose rhyming *The History of the Rebellion* was to be published in Glasgow later that year, recalls the arrival of the Highlanders:

To Glasgow they came the next day
In a very poor *forlorn* way [*neglected*]
The shot was rusted in the gun
Their swords from *scabbards* would not *twin* [*sheath*] [*separate*]
Their *countenance* fierce as a wild bear [*look, expression*]
Out o'er their eyes hung down their hair. . . .
Their beards were turned black and brown
The like was ne'er seen in that town
Some of them did barefooted run
Minded no *mire* nor stony groun'; [*mud*]
But when shaven, dressed and clothed again
They turned to be like other men.
Eight days they did in Glasgow rest
Until they were all clothed and dressed.
Graham, History, 123–4

Glasgow had no sympathy for the Jacobite cause. Very few Glasgow men had joined them (see page 15). Before the Highland army set out for England, they forced Glasgow to pay them £5000. On their return they expected the people in the city to feed them and give them shelter. They also needed new clothes and the city had to supply '12000 shirts, 6000 bonnets, 6000 pair shoes, 6000 waistcoats at 4/– [20p] per yard [nearly 1 metre], 6000 pair stockings.'

Then Prince Charles inspected his whole army on Glasgow Green:

It was the first general review he had made since he left the Highlands. Hitherto he had carefully concealed his weakness. Now, thinking himself sure of doubling his army in a few days, he was not unwilling to let the world see with what a handful of men he had penetrated so far into England and retired almost without any loss.
Maxwell, Narrative, 90

10 Where now, Highland Soldier?

While the Highland army was in England both sides, Government and Jacobite, were trying to recruit more soldiers in the Highlands. It happened that the chief judge in Scotland (the Lord President of the Court of Session), was Duncan Forbes of Culloden, who had an estate not far from Inverness. He had great influence over many of the Highland chiefs. He had the idea of offering Highlanders the chance to enlist to fight for the government. The more men he could attract, the fewer would join Prince Charles.

From Glasgow the Highland army moved to Stirling. They took the town and began to lay siege to the Castle. Here their new recruits came in, Frasers, Farquharsons and Gordons, Mackintoshes and Mackenzies, to bring the Jacobite force up to over 8 000 men, far bigger than it had ever been before. Meanwhile the British army in Scotland under its new commander, General Hawley, marched to Falkirk. Hawley reckoned he had 2 000 more men than Prince Charles, enough to crush this Jacobite rebellion once and for all.

1. How did Duncan Forbes try to stop some Highlanders fighting for Prince Charles?

2. What evidence is there here that more men joined Prince Charles?

The Battle of Falkirk

As at Prestonpans, it was the Jacobite army under Lord George Murray who took the initiative. They advanced speedily to take up a commanding position on Falkirk Muir and Hawley had to send three regiments of dragoons to stop them. The horsemen came on in the driving rain. The Highlanders, muskets at the ready, held their fire. They waited, and waited, until the horses were twelve, ten paces away from them. Suddenly they fired. The effect was shattering. Many of the horsemen fell dead; the rest took to flight. Drawing their swords, the Highlanders charged the supporting foot soldiers, who also turned and ran. Only on the right did Hawley's men have any success. Both armies became impossible to control because so many of the men were rushing helter-skelter in retreat or pursuit. John Home who was taken prisoner by the Highlanders in this battle described the scene like this:

The field of battle presented a spectacle seldom seen in war. Part of the King's army, much the greater part, was flying to the eastward, and part of the rebel army was flying to the westward. The presence of Charles encouraged the Highlanders. Ordering them to follow him, he led them to the

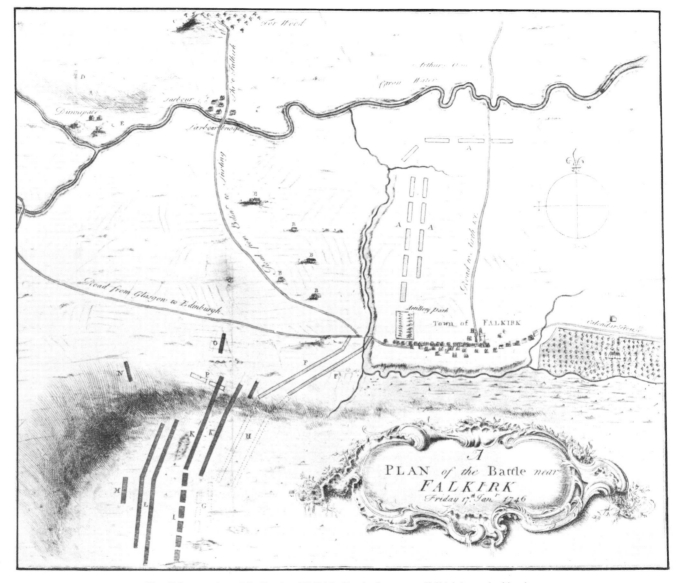

Detail from a plan of the Battle of Falkirk. Hawley's camp at Falkirk is marked by As.
The battle took place on the higher ground (on the bottom left of the plan).
L and M show the Highlanders, I Hawley's dragoons and K his foot soldiers
(reprinted by permission of the Scottish United Services Museum)

brow of the hill. Before it grew dark, General Hawley gave orders to set fire to the tents [in his own camp], and marching his army through the town of Falkirk, retreated to Linlithgow, leaving behind him seven pieces of cannon, with a great quantity of provision, ammunition and baggage.

Home, *History*, 173–5

1. *Who did so much to keep chiefs and clansmen loyal to the Government?*
2. *(a) How many men did Prince Charles have now?*
   (b) How many had he at the Battle of Prestonpans? (See Workguide No. 7.)
   (c) How many men did General Hawley say were under his command before the Battle of Falkirk?
3. *Why did John Home say this battle was so unusual?*
4. *What did General Hawley do that shows he knew he had lost the battle?*
   (This is a good time to turn to No. 1 in Workguide No. 10.)

The battle over, Prince Charles turned his attention again to the siege of Stirling Castle. He did not realise that so many of his men were deserting him. The chiefs told him how serious it was in this letter:

29th January 1746

We are certain that a vast number of soldiers are gone home since the Battle of Falkirk. This evil is increasing hourly and not in our power to prevent. If the enemy should march [against us], we can foresee nothing but utter destruction to the few that will remain, considering the inequality of our numbers to that of the enemy. We are humbly of opinion that there is no way out of the danger but by retiring immediately to the Highlands. In spring an army of ten thousand effective Highlanders can be brought together and will follow your R.H. wherever you think proper.

The hard marches which your army have undergone, the winter season, and now, the inclemency [*harshness*] of the weather, cannot fail of making this measure approved of by your Royal Highness's allies abroad as well as your faithful adherents [*supporters*] at home. The greatest difficulty that occurs to us is the saving of the artillery, particularly the heavy cannon. Better some of these were thrown into the River Forth as that your R.H., besides the danger of your own person, should risk the flower of your army, which must inevitably [*certainly*] be the case, if this retreat be not agreed to and gone about without the loss of one moment. . . .

Signed by
    Lord George Murray
    Lochiel
    Keppoch
    Clanranald
    Ardsheal
    Lochgarry
    Scothouse
    Simon Fraser, Master of Lovat

Home, *History*, 352–4

The Jacobites did withdraw to the north, the clans going with the Prince by Dunkeld through the Highlands to Inverness, the others taking the lower, but longer, road round by Aberdeen. Many men got the chance to go home for a time and some did not come back. Government troops, now under the command of the Duke of Cumberland, came north in force to Aberdeen.

Stirling Castle
(from an engraving made in 1791)   37

11 The Last Battle

A soldier from the 1st or Royal Regiment of Foot (detail from *1742 Cloathing Book, reprinted by permission of the Scottish United Services Museum*)

The Two Sides

The King's Army

At their base in Aberdeen the soldiers in the King's army trained and drilled as they waited for spring to return. There were nine thousand of them in all. Some belonged to regiments who had turned and run away at Falkirk; some were in regiments just back from fighting in Europe.

They were strong in cavalry, whose job it was to scout ahead on their horses and guard the wings when the army was on the move. In battle, too, they protected the wings and could be sent round the side of the enemy lines ready to attack and pursue. The gunners practised and practised to gain speed in loading and firing their cannon. These guns could hurl either three pound iron shot or grapeshot, a mass of smaller shot and bits of iron—deadly weapons the Highlanders had not had to face in earlier battles. But most of the men were infantry, and they were training to stand against the Highland charge with broadsword and target, and win. In his victories the Highland soldier had used his wooden shield to protect his left side and had his right arm free to slash or jab with his sword. The Redcoat foot-soldiers were learning a new method to fight against him: each man was to use his bayonet, not against the man in front of him, but against the unprotected side of the man to his right. Their trade was war and they were kept to it by the lash and the threat of a hanging. In return, they were properly clothed and could rely on being regularly paid and fed.

In early April, their commander-in-chief, William, Duke of Cumberland, who had pursued the Highlanders all the way from Derby, marched his army towards Inverness, where his cousin Prince Charles was. His men needed a victory over the Highlanders now to regain their pride in themselves as professional soldiers. As George II's son, Cumberland knew that the safety of his father's crown depended upon his men winning the coming battle. He was young to be a general but had gained experience in Flanders and was a careful and methodical commander.

On 15th April he rested his army for the day at Nairn, fifteen miles from Inverness. From the supply ships which accompanied him off-shore he had ample ammunition and food given to every man. He was twenty-five that day and he gave every man a special issue of brandy to celebrate his birthday. Tomorrow they would probably fight.

The Jacobite Army

When it was discovered that the Redcoats were advancing, messengers were sent to tell the scattered clan regiments to gather at Inverness without delay. Some came very quickly, others were unwilling to come.

'Many of our people, as it was seed time, had slipped home.'
Murray, *Marches*, 120

Many were discontented because of lack of pay and the shortage of food. 13 000 gold coins sent to Prince Charles from France never reached him, and as Dougal Graham recalls:

They had no meal, mutton or beef
Of cheese and butter no relief;
The cry among them night and day,
Was, *Give me money, meat or pay*
Graham, *History*, 157

On 15th April, when Cumberland's soldiers were resting and celebrating at Nairn, most of the Highlanders had only a biscuit to eat all day, and some did not even have that. There may have been as many as five thousand men in their army the following day; there were certainly no more. Of these, few were cavalry and almost none were trained gunners. They had few cannon and these were of different sizes, and the men who manned them discovered they had very little ammunition.

The Highlanders had won victories at Prestonpans and Falkirk even when the odds were stacked against them. Thanks to the element of surprise in the tactics of Lord George Murray, their commander, they had fought these battles in a way which suited them, and prevented the enemy from employing their superior numbers or equipment to advantage. When the armies met on the bare and flat Culloden Moor, Murray might complain (and he did) that it was not good ground for Highlanders to fight on, but he was not in charge this time. Prince Charles had decided that, for the first time in his life, he would command his army himself. (You should answers questions 1 and 2 on Workguide 11 before reading on.)

To try to take the King's army by surprise it was decided to attack their camp at Nairn before daybreak. Unfortunately, the Highlanders made such slow progress that they did not reach Nairn before it began to grow light. The camp was alert, and the attack was abandoned. There was nothing for it but to turn back to Culloden where,

'everybody seemed to think of nothing but sleep. The men were prodigiously tired with hunger and fatigue. Vast numbers of them went into Inverness and the villages about, both to sleep and pick up what little nourishment they could get. About two hours later, the officers ordered the drums to beat and the pipes to play, which alarm caused great hurry and confusion amongst people half dead with fatigue.'
Elcho, 428–9

Jacobite piper
(reconstruction)

The Battle

The Duke of Cumberland

Cumberland's army was coming. The Highlanders were hastily drawn up by O'Sullivan, one of Prince Charles' Irish officers, to be ready for them. They stood in a line, with each clan forming a separate group. They faced north-east and had a wall to their right. The battle began with the thunder of cannon:

[Cumberland's gunners] charged their cannon with grapeshot and as they were well pointed, they did great execution. The Highlanders had orders not to move until the word of command to advance was given them and then they were to give their fire very near, draw their swords and rush in. They suffered the cannonade very impatiently, a great many threw themselves down flat upon the ground, and some, but few, gave way and ran off. The Duke's army detached 600 Campbells and a squadron of dragoons to see and flank [*attack the side of*] the Prince's right wing. The Duke's army kept a continuous fire both of cannon and musketry which killed a vast number of the Prince's people.

The Mackintoshes were the first to advance, inclining to the right. At last, the word of command to advance was given and all the line moved forward, but the whole left wing gave way. The centre joined the right, and in a sort of a mob, broke the regiments opposite to them in the first line but the second line marching up beat them off. As the Campbells had taken possession of the park walls on the right, they [the charging Highlanders] received several flank fires which killed and destroyed great numbers of them. In the attack upon the right many of the Highlanders were killed with bayonets, and it was the more easy as they had no targets, for they would not be at the pains upon a march to carry them.

Elcho, 431–4

The two armies at Culloden. On the right are the regiments of the British army, lettered *a* to *p* in three lines, with the Campbells and dragoons moving round from A to DD. Facing them, the clans numbered 1 to 22 advanced from BB to CC and then gave way (Note the 'Observations' which appeared in a corner of the original map.)

Observations.

The Highlanders had been without pay, and scarce of provisions for some weeks.

They were obliged to fight, after a fatiguing march, without any refreshment: having had no sleep and but little food the two days and nights immediately preceeding: and wanting numbers of their men, who were dispers'd in the adjacent villages on these accounts.

It was but a small number of them, (that were present,) did actually engage, the others being intimidated on seeing those who made such a desperate attack, obliged to give way.

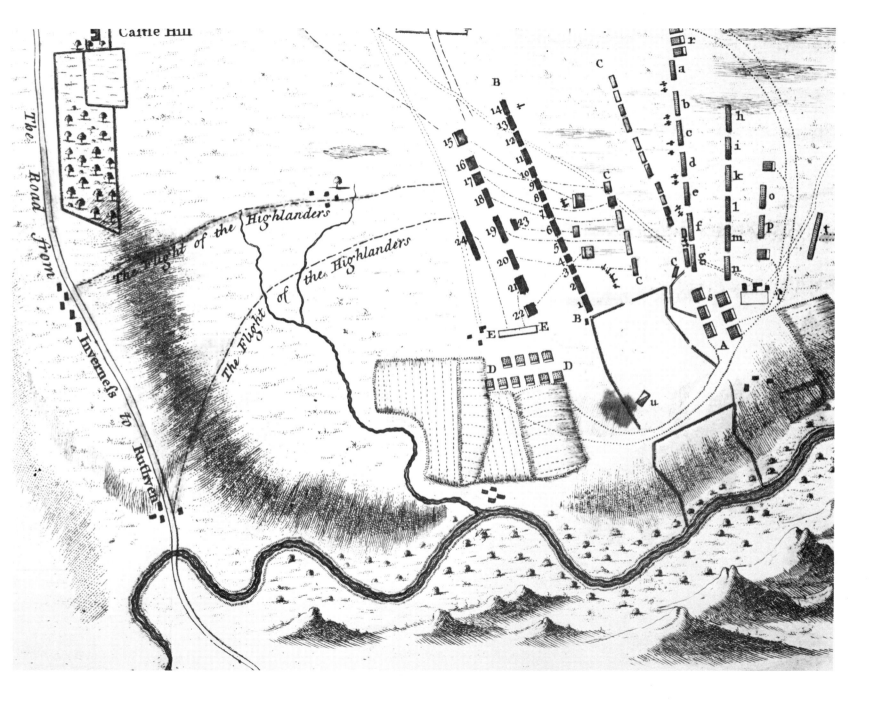

Castle Hill

The Road from Invernefs to Ruthven

The Flight of the Highlanders

The Flight of the Highlanders

B
14
13
12
15
16
11
17
10
18
9
8
24
23
7
19
6
20
5
21
4
3
22
2
1

C

C

C
B

E E

D D

r
a
b
c
d
e
f
g

h
i
k
l
m
n

o
p

t

s

A

u

1. *Which branch of his army did Cumberland use first?*
2. *What effect did it have on the Highlanders?*
3. *What did Cumberland ask the Campbells and the cavalry to do?*
4. *Which happened first —*
   (a) the Mackintoshes advanced, or
   (b) the word of command was given to advance?
5. *From which two directions were men shooting at the charging Highlanders?*
6. *Why were so many killed at close quarters?*

The picture on page 43 shows the British infantry meeting the Highlanders charging against them. It was painted by David Morier soon after the battle and is very accurate, partly because he was able to use Jacobite prisoners as models.

Like the earlier battles in the 'Forty-five, the fighting at Culloden did not last long. It was all over in half an hour. The cavalry were pursuing the retreating Highlanders and Prince Charles was led away from the moor. He had lost the last battle.

A View from Each Side

'How We Won' by an Englishman with Cumberland's army:

Inverness, 16th April

At last we have done it.—The Rebels have met this day with a confounded drubbing.—The Duke and all our generals are well. Lord Robert Kerr is wounded.—Colonel Rich has lost his left hand.—Captain Grosset, I am told, is among the slain.—Our loss otherwise is very inconsiderable. Of the rebels are a d - - - n'd number killed, and an innumerable number of prisoners. Among the last is Lord Kilmarnock, Lord Lewis Gordon and John Murray, etc.

Edinburgh Evening Courant, April 21

Why We Lost—extracts from a letter from Lord George Murray to Prince Charles:

Ruthven, 19 April

May it please your Royal Highness,

Sir, you will I hope pardon me if I mention a few truths which all the gentlemen of our army seem convinced of;

It was highly wrong to have set up the royal standard without [knowing that] his most Christian Majesty, the King of France, would assist you with all his force.

Mr. O'Sullivan, whom you trusted, committed gross blunders. He did not so much as visit the ground where we were to be drawn up in line of battle. It was a fatal error to allow the enemy so fair a field for their horse and cannon. Never was more improper ground for Highlanders than that where we fought.

The want of provisions was another misfortune. The three last days [before the battle] our army was starved.

If we had got plenty of provisions we might have crossed the water of Nairn [river on map, page 41] and by the strength of our position made it so dangerous for the enemy to have attacked us that they would not have ventured to have done it. We would have done by the enemy as they have unhappily done by us.

Your Royal Highness knows I have no design to continue in the army.

I am with great zeal

Your R.H.'s most dutiful and humble servant

George Murray.

Blaikie, *Itinerary*, 79–80

'An incident in the Rebellion of 1745' by David Morier (*reproduced by gracious permission of Her Majesty the Queen*)

12 Celebrations in the South: Cruelties in the North

Public Rejoicing

As soon as people heard about the victory of the King's army at Culloden, celebrations began all over England and the Lowlands of Scotland. The newspapers published reports of what people did in different places. Here are two examples, one from Eyemouth, a little fishing village on the coast of Berwickshire, the other from Glasgow, where the Highlanders had not been welcome guests earlier.

Eyemouth

The Minister, with the principal inhabitants, assembled round a covered table in the middle of the town, the whole populace [*all the people*] surrounding them, and public thanks being first offered up to Almighty God, the following healths [*toasts*] were pronounced aloud and drunk by all the company:

A Health to his sacred Majesty, King George, and to the utter extinction [*death*] of Jacobitism.

A Health to H.R.H. Frederick, Prince of Wales and disappointment to the designs [*plans*] of the Pretender.

A Health to H.R.H. William, Duke of Cumberland and to the entire reduction [*overthrow*] of rebellious subjects and foreign enemies.

A large bonfire blazed the whole evening and at each Health a discharge of small arms [*muskets, pistols*] proclaimed the public joy.

Glasgow

At ten in the forenoon the music bells were played and a large bonfire was lighted at the Cross. In the afternoon, the whole bells of the City were rung. The magistrates, the gentlemen of the University and principal inhabitants of the City, went to the top of the stair leading to the Town's great hall where they drank (under a discharge of firearms by the Town's regiment) the Health of His Majesty, their Royal Highnesses the Prince and Princess of Wales, the Duke of Cumberland, etc.

In the evening the whole windows of the City were splendidly illuminated and the night concluded with great expressions of joy.

1. *Who took the lead in the celebrations in (a) Eyemouth, and (b) Glasgow?*
2. *What did they do first in (a) Eyemouth, and (b) Glasgow?*
3. *Whose healths were drunk in both places?*
4. *What did Eyemouth want to happen to:*
   (a) Jacobite feeling;
   (b) Prince Charles' plans;
   (c) the rebels?

Cruelties in the North

To people in the south, Cumberland and his soldiers became heroes because they had crushed the clansmen who were in rebellion against the King. But in the weeks that followed their victory at Culloden, these soldiers ranged through the Highland glens to make it clear that they were the new masters. They killed and plundered and wilfully destroyed; they burned homes, they drove off people's cattle. The Highlands became a wasteland full of suffering and sorrow, even for people who had had nothing to do with the recent rebellion.

How they took over the town of Inverness can be gathered from this letter in which the magistrates look for help from Duncan Forbes of Culloden, the Lord President of the Court of Session:

They have quartered [*lodged*] themselves officers, soldiers, servants, wives, horses and dogs. Their officers do all feed together in messes [*places where soldiers eat together*] in private houses, which requires all the conveniences of the houses, kitchen, furniture, etc. They have taken our Town Hall and Town Clerk's office. We have no Tolbooth courthouse or prison. The soldiers generally are the greatest rogues in the British army. They have taken away all the timber that could be found, gates and doors from gardens and all the old houses, even a door of the Church. They have carried off ploughs and plough-irons out of the cornfields and corn from cornyards. Our town is reduced to the greatest misery for lack of fire and meal. No inhabitant dare buy a cart of peats in the market. Meal coming to market is carried off ere [*before*] it reaches the Meal House. An inhabitant can't get a grain unless there's enough to satisfy the soldiers' immediate demands, which rarely happens.

More Culloden Papers, vol. V, 129

Study the account above then rewrite and complete the following sentences:

1. *Some people could not use their own houses because .... were .... in them.*
2. *People could not cook or keep warm because soldiers took all the .... and ....*
3. *They were starving because the .... of the soldiers for .... came first. .*
4. *It was cold in Church because a .... was missing.*
5. *With no .... and a shortage of ...., it would be difficult to grow crops next year.*

Choose from: soldiers, peats, demands, living, door, seed, ploughs, meal, timber.

There are so many accounts of cruelty by the troops, that a case when mercy was shown is so unusual it is worth noting. Here is one, described in a letter from General John Campbell to the wife of Stewart of Ardsheal, who had led the Stewarts at Culloden.

Appin, May 25th, 1746

Madam,

The unhappy situation Ardsheal has brought you and your innocent children into by being so deeply concerned in this unnatural rebellion makes my heart ache. I know the King to be compassionate and merciful. I know the brave Duke under whose command and orders *I* act, to have as much humanity [*kindness*] as any man on earth. I have therefore taken the liberty of *ordering back* your milk cows, six sheep and as many lambs. I have ordered two bolls of meal out of my own stores to be left here for you, which I desire you to accept for the use of yourself and little ones. I entreat you to bring up your children to be good subjects of his Majesty. I wish your husband, by surrendering himself to the Duke of Cumberland, had given me an opportunity of recommending him to his Majesty's mercy, I feel for you and am, Madam,

    Your most obedient and humble servant
        John Campbell.

The Stewarts of Appin, 139

1. (a) Who was 'the brave Duke'?
   (b) Do the actions of his men suggest that their commander was as kind as any man on earth?
2. (a) What is John Campbell doing that is so unusual?
   (b) Could he possibly have had any other motive, other than kindness?
(Note: Stewart of Ardsheal was still in hiding.)

In September, Stewart of Ardsheal landed safely in France. In the winter other soldiers arrived and drove out his wife and young children from their home, looted it and knocked it down. The family fled to a hut, where her sixth child was born. Then soldiers came and chased them out again, to try to find some other shelter in the snow.

In the south, people had been happy when they heard that the rebels had been defeated at Culloden, but did they know how much the Highland people were made to suffer once it was over?

A 'wanted' poster put out for Prince Charles offering a reward of £30 000 to anyone who captured him

13 How Did People Know Then?

Ours is an age of instant news. Whatever happens of importance anywhere in the world is brought to our attention almost immediately by pictures on the television screen, the sound of radio and the printed word in the daily papers. Compared with this, eighteenth century people knew far less about what was happening and their knowledge was limited to a much smaller local area.

Word of Mouth

News travelled no faster than the people who carried it and was often out-of-date by the time people heard it. It was usually passed on by word of mouth and changed a lot in the telling. What people heard and believed to be true could be only partly true and occasionally it was completely untrue. It often depended on who was relating the news. People in a Highland glen, for example, would hear a different story from a clan recruiting party than from a group of deserters about how their men in the Jacobite army were faring.

Letters

News also travelled by letter. Both sides realised early in the 'Forty-five that there was information in letters which they would like to see. The only way was to open letters and read them. A man who did this for the Jacobites in Dundee is mentioned in Chapter 3. Of course, there was no time or opportunity to open every letter, and since some of those left unopened might contain plans or instructions useful to the enemy, it seemed wise to delay all the mail. Far more letters were written during the 'Forty-five than were ever received.

Newspapers

Of the people who could read, not many could afford to buy newspapers. The Edinburgh papers, the *Caledonian Mercury* and the *Evening Courant*, cost less than 1p each. They were single sheets folded in half to make four sides, or pages, and were subject to stamp duty. Much of the news in them was quite old. The *Caledonian Mercury* on Monday 21st April, for example, carried a report on page 2 of Cumberland's army in Aberdeen being about to set off for Inverness on the 8th, nearly a fortnight earlier. But when something important took place, efforts were made to spread the news quickly. The battle of Culloden happened on Wednesday, 16th April. On the following Saturday night the news reached Edinburgh. On the Sunday, Edinburgh people knew that *something* had happened, something pleasing to the soldiers in the Castle, because at 2 o'clock in the

The Caledonian Mercury.

Num. 3987

Edinburgh, Thursday, May 1, 1746.

From the London Gazette, April 26.

Whitehall, April 26, 1746.
This Afternoon a Messenger arrived from the Duke of Cumberland, with the following Particulars of the Victory obtained by his Royal Highness over the Rebels, on Wednesday the 16th instant near Culloden.

Inverness, April 18.

ON Tuesday the 15th the Rebels burnt Fort Augustus, which convinced us of their Resolution to stand an Engagement with the King's Troops. We gave our Men a Day's Halt at Nairn, and on the 16th marched from thence, between 4 and 5, in four Columns. The three Lines of Foot (reckoning the Reserve for one) were broken into three from the Right, which made the three Columns equal, and each of five Battalions. The Artillery and Baggage followed the first Column on the Right, and the Cavalry made the 4th Column. After we had marched

upon the Right, where his R. Highness had placed himself, imagining the greatest Push would be there, they came down three several Times within 100 Yards of our Men, firing their Pistols and brandishing their Swords; but the Royals and Pulteney's hardly took their Firelocks from their Shoulders, so that after those faint Attempts they made off; and the little Squadrons on our Right were sent to pursue them. Gen. Hawley had, by the Help of our Highlanders, beat down two little Stone-walls, and came in upon the right Flank of their second Line.

As their whole first Line came down to attack at once, their Right somewhat out-flanked Barrel's Regiment, which was our Left, and the greatest Part of the little Loss we sustained was there; but Bligh's and Sempil's giving a Fire upon those who had out-flanked Barrel's, soon repulsed them, and Barrel's Regiment and Monro's fairly ...

... in the ... ... who were at Inverness the Day of the Battle of Culloden, to Major Gen. Bland. SIR, *Inverness, April 16.*
THE French Officers and Soldiers, who are at Inverness, surrender themselves Prisoners to his Royal Highness the Duke of Cumberland, and hope for every thing which is to be expected from the English Generosity.
Sign'd *Cusack, Murphy, Le Marquis de Guilles, Debau, d'Ubrien, M'Donald.*
To the Commanding Officer of the Troops of his R. Highness the Duke of Cumberland.
Translation of the Parole signed by the Officers in the Service of his most Christian Majesty, with their Names, Titles, &c. *Inverness, April 17. 1746.*
WE the underwritten, in the Service of his most Christian Majesty, acknowledge ourselves Prisoners of War of his Britannick Majesty; and we engage ourselves upon our Parole of Honour, not to go out of the Town of Inverness, without a Permission from his Royal Highness Duke of Cumberland. In Witness whereof, ... have thereunto set the Seal of ... d Quarters at Inverness,

... of the Royal Scots.

Return of the Rebel Officers now Prisoners in Inverness, April 19. 1746.

Colonel Lord Kilmarnock.
3 { Colonel Francis Farquharson.
Colonel Mac Lachlan.
1 Major, James Stuart.
Captain James Farquharson,
Ditto, Andrew Wood.
5 { Ditto, Alexander Coming.
Ditto, Sprewell.
Ditto, Alexander Buchannan.
1 Lieutenant George Gordon.
Ensign Duncan Mac Greggor.
3 { Ditto, James Lindsay.
Ditto, James Hay.
1 Engineer, John Finlayson
1 Chaplain George Law
1 Deputy Pay-master, ——— Nairn.
1 Surgeon, George Lowther.
1 Surgeon, John Rothery.
1 Life-Guard, Sir John Wedderburn.

Return of Ordnance and Stores taken at and since the Battle of Culloden. Inverness, April 10.
Ordnanc ... 1 lb. ¼ ——— 3

morning the Castle guns fired, and were answered by the guns of the warships at Leith. On its page 3 on 21st April, the *Mercury* carried its first printed report of the battle:

There has been an engagement on Wednesday near Inverness betwixt the Army under his Royal Highness the Duke, and the rebels in which the latter have been defeat[ed]. Some hundreds were killed, several taken prisoners, and those who escaped have retired to the mountains.

Notice that this was not front page news, and that no headlines were used. The only headings were the names of the places news came from. News from Europe being considered more important than home news, it was usually on page 1, and London news came before Edinburgh news.

The *Caledonian Mercury* was different on May 1st, however; every one of its pages was about the battle of Culloden, a fortnight after it happened.

Excerpts from a newspaper report of the Battle of Culloden